ISBN - 978 - 0 - 95485

Published by:
Zebra Publishing
7 Gosforth Terrace
South Gosforth
Newcastle upon Tyne
NE3 1RT

For information contact
jeff@zebrapublishing.co.uk

Copyright © Simma
Cover image © Owen Davies

Printed and bound by:
Jasprint
Washington
Co Durham

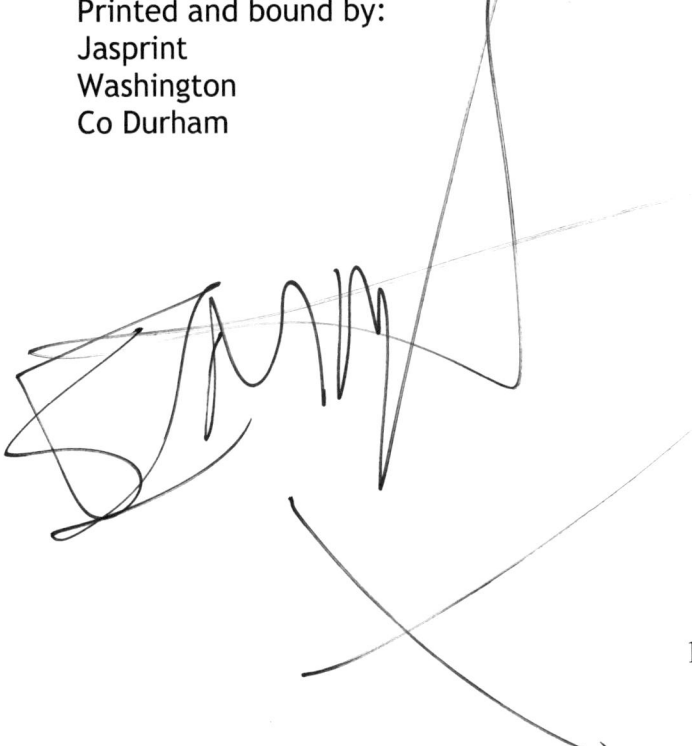

Last Night I Married the Audience

Simma

Foreword

Everyone knows Simma is a fabulous singer songwriter with a way of rousing a crowd and raising a roof only the best entertainers have. But when I would say to him, as we chatted over lattes and Dr Who plots that he was also a stand up comedian and a poet, he disagreed for years.

Now that his book of wonderful stand up poetry is out, I feel I can be quite justified in saying "Told you so". His timing, wit, precision and playfulness with words and ability to make more connections than an electrician with a sonic screwdriver make him a compelling writer. The pleasure he takes in crafting a piece, structuring it, and fashioning gold nuggets into credit crunch beating bling pays off brilliantly.

It's a fascinating process- performing in front of an audience and Simma has all the elements needed to make it a high art- the way you have to be part salesperson, conductor, psychiatrist, amplifier, speaker, fool and wiseman.

He's had a glorious honeymoon as a working artist and perhaps this book is the gift he's giving to the world for the first anniversary-paper. I know that his talent, energy and enthusiasm will take his poetry through many more. For now, enjoy the shining, many faceted diamonds of poems from this master communicator.

Kate Fox

Introduction

It's been a very strange and gratifying journey since it was first suggested that I should put together a collection of poems for publication. I was surprised and slightly terrified at the idea, but with a lot of encouragement and perseverance, this book was born.

I'll spare you the obvious "Lad from the West End of Newcastle goes against all stereotypes and becomes poet" spiel, as I'm sure you can fill in those gaps, and life isn't actually like Billy Elliot or The Full Monty. I started writing poetry long before I called myself a poet, though. In fact that came much, much later, and only at the insistence of the inspirational Kate Fox. That said, words have always been my living. Doing odd things with language, whether as a salesman, a songwriter, radio presenter or compère, has kept me alive.

I'm immensely grateful to Zebra Publishing for offering me this opportunity to present these poems to you. I feel like this is a coming together of lots of the work I've done so far, I'm really excited that it's arrived, and I hope you enjoy it. You're the audience, after all.

Simma

Acknowledgements

This book Is dedicated To Tony Battle

Special thanks to the people who helped to inspire this book,

The Audience, Acoustic Circus, Alan Hull, Annie Moir, Danny Ward, Dan Walsh, Dr. Elizabeth Anslow, Ella Burbridge, Jeff Price, Jo Casey & Family, Kate Fox, Lindisfarne, Morris Rodham, Naomi Woodward, Nev Clay, Owen Davies, Peter Burbridge, Rod Clements, Simon Hoban, Dr. Stephanie Bell, Steve Daggett, The Buskers, The Rvd. Andy Mackin, Verity Burton, and everyone who I couldn't fit onto this list

Contents

8. Last Night I Married The Audience

9. Set Up Train

10. The Elephants of Irrelevance

12. Singer

14. Cheese

15. Looking for Work

16. Mustn't Grumble

18. LP

19. More than Music (moment of madness)

20. Inevitable

21. Anti-Sonnet

22. Smoking Poem

23. One Night Two and Half Weeks in

24. Break up Calypso

25. Ode to Angry Environmentalist Poet

26. Note to Self – List of things not to write poems about

28. On Me Head

30. See Vee

31. Compère

32. Heated Conversation (an exercise in backwards masking)

33. James at the Job Centre

34. On Beginnings

35. Automatic for the People

36. The Day you Decided

38. Old Friends

39. Height / Polite

40. Have a Good Show

41. Highland Conversation

42. The Drink

43. Stop Kidding Yourself

44. Daytime in Darlo

45. One Down

46. Meeting the Public

48. Reality / Television

49. The Committee

50. Secret Track

51. Physicians of Penzance

52. Judge Dread

54. Backbone

Last Night I Married The Audience

Arriving, we avoid eye contact with each other
then, first, nervous glances, nods
the edgy ambiguity of the nearly-smile

We've both done this many times before
will tonight be the one?
that special, singular, extraordinary meeting?

Settling in we nervously socialise
did I wear the right thing?
I smile, introduce myself and sing

My first songs are quiet, gentle and sweet
anxious to show you my sensitive side
I'm not like those other acts, I'm special

You react beautifully, engaged and enthused
time to pick up the pace
I begin to carry you, not quite running yet

Songs you know, sparking memories of childhood
now I'm really pushing your buttons
remember this? I understand you, I know you

We laugh with each other, and now we're running
through fields of half-remembered lyrics
yes, you love me! I knew you would! I could tell

In-between songs we communicate our affection
you support me, I make you laugh
I still love you; it's not all about the applause but

You do expect a lot from me now
hit after hit after hit after hit and
you're drinking too much, are you listening to me?

I can still get through to you - I still hear
but only when we're both shouting
you don't understand me anymore and I'm tired

Nobody wanted it to end, it just did
goodnight and a safe journey home
you shout "more!" but we both know it's over

We had a great run you and I
I hope I see you around but
tomorrow night I'm meeting someone else

Set Up Train

Speakers and cables
and moving of tables
the floor seems unstable
and back to the van
placing of bases
and basses on stages
microphones, cases
and back to the van
lighting and candles
bags with snapped handles
these leads are a shambles!
and back to the van

STOP!

Beer…

stands for Music
stands for Speakers
stands for Lighting
stands for Mics
stands for Guitars
stands for Keyboards
stands for Cymbals
stands for Drums
this is what we stand for

Tuners and Instruments
mystery Implements
this bit of kit's intricate
back to the van
MP3s, Batteries
unlabelled DVDs
I don't know what's on these
back to the van
that speaker needs moving
lifting confusion
percussive contusion
OW! Back to the van
now plugging it all in
the late acts are calling
with excuses appalling
so exhausted and falling
we lock up the van

Eyes closed and defying noise round me
now we've emptied our equipment and energy
I hear a faint voice say
drink up and get ready
here's the audience, it's time to start work

The Elephants Of Irrelevance

We're no good for each other
it's obvious to see
we're badly suited, mismatched
we're uneven, you and me

We add nothing to each other
how can I explain?
the appropriate simile is
locked in my brain

We're useless to each other
we're like

a marmoset with a clarinet
a Persian cat with a cricket bat
a llama with a banana
a hake with a cake
lying on the bakery floor
wishing he hadn't told anyone
it was his birthday

Like a sheep in a jeep
a chinchilla with weed killer
a sparrow with a barrow
a beaver with a cleaver
there aren't any butchers
within travelling distance of the dam
anyway, he's got sharp teeth

Like meerkats with beer mats
a Stork with a fork
a pig in a wig
a kangaroo with a portaloo
he can't reach the handle
his arms are to short
and he likes using the bush

Like a pike with a bike
a lion with a tie on
a dragonfly with a chicken pie
a Hippo with a Zippo
he has no thumbs
it keeps getting wet
and he's really trying to give up

Like a leopard with a shepherd
a puma with a tumour
a giraffe with a carafe
a pigeon with religion
the other birds
have no organised belief system
so are impossible to convert

Like a homebody gorilla
with a time share in a villa
like a philistine koala
with tickets for la Scala
like a grizzly bear
with a conference pear

We're the elephants of irrelevance, you and I
want to give it one more try?

Singer

I've always been a singer
ever since I can remember
I recall a nasty kid saying
"why are you always singing?"

It's got a ring to it, "singer"
sounds like a job if you say it properly
people will accept it as respectable
a career, even for someone like me

But now I am a poet
It's the same, people keep saying
It isn't, I proudly announce
and wait for your reaction

Are ye ganna write aall
like Geordie Poems an' that kinda thing
like aall aboot Newcastle 'n' that?
write aboot Shearer, or Jackie Milburn
people love that, eee, wor bairn loves that
not that ees Fatha would let him read poems like!
so are ye deein like, Geordie poems n that?

No

I thought I could write universal poems
eternal themes, separation and loss
how the shortest distance can become insurmountable
if you build barriers instead of bridges

Eee, you could write aboot the bridges
on the quayside, ee, a love the bridges
write about the new one
ye might get a grant if ye write about the new one
de ye get paid, like, when ya doin, bein a poet?
waste of government money I reckon
The' could be building houses wi that money

No

I work in horrible bars for grasping landlords
make ends meet and get the work where I can

Have ye gorra job like?
I mean like a job, though?
my Mickey works in Kwik Save, I could gerrim to ask for ye
Ye could write a poem aboot it!
what rhymes wi kwik save, howay!

No

I don't need a job, I have a job
I'm a singer, I sing in bars

Eee, d'ye sing like Geordie songs 'n' that
Dance Te The Daddy, Cushie Butterfield?
a love aall them, an Fog on the Tyne?
D'ye sing Fog on the Tyne?

Yes
Yes I do

Cheese

When I play a certain type of song
poppy, happy, bright and familiar
people call it "cheese"

Musicians say it in a derogatory way
as if to put down these ready-diced, chopped
pre-packed slices of song

They turn their noses up at these tunes
the ones drunken punters devour hungrily
on Saturday nights, otherwise starved of entertainment

Why anyone would defame the name
of something so enjoyed by so many
frankly, leaves me baffled

I've always found cheese strangely satisfying
filling and tasty in an everyday way
if a little self-indulgent

Looking For Work

Stepping out of the beating rain
I pace down the rattling gravel
1-2-3-4
the door slams like a snare
the shock of it jangles my nerves
a bell above the door announces me
with a friendly two-note melody

Alerted to the appearance of a non-regular
the pub dog barks his song of disapproval
1-2-3-4
the glass and china cymbals
keep chaotic time around me
knives on plates clatter joy
like rehearsals for Chinese New Year

The conversation hums and drones
the bandit thuds a sudden payout
1-2-3-4
one voice, then two, then a choir
of laughter peals through the bar
and I, pianissimo
ask if I can speak to the boss

I compose myself as I wait
hear him thump down big bass stairs
1-2-3-4
I smile, raise my voice
enthusiastically give him the pitch
but his face, dark as a Wagner overture
shows he already has the measure of me

"Sorry," he says, "We don't do music here"

Mustn't Grumble

Sometimes they even say it to your face
"It's ok for you, try doing my job
I despise my job and I have no choice
it's easy for you, tunes, beer and applause
oh what a hardship! you should work in my
shop, office, lab, site, café, classroom, bar"

I try to reply without sounding pleased
that I love my work, don't work for pennies
for people I hate, don't get up early
I say to myself- right, be positive
accentuate things I love about life
be upbeat and smile, don't forget to smile!

but it's going wrong! the more I love mine
the more he hates his. I try hard to keep
upbeat, smiling - perpetually smiling
'cos if the singer isn't smiling, then
what chance of happy does he ever have?
it's performance, but my mask breaks halfway

It's great
yeah, really, it's great
playing and singing
truly, can't complain
except for the hours
the hours are awful

and the lack of security of course
not knowing where the next gig's coming from
and, you know, some landlords are difficult
herd of money-grabbing swine, actually
and the punters! pickled in their own juice
shouting the same requests every night

bloody Hotel sodding California
and Sweet Home bleedin' Alabama
when the furthest they've been in their whole lives
is the caravan or Butlins in Rhyl
The toll it takes on your hands and throat
the complete lack of holidays, sick time

all this and the nerves, the travelling
never being able to spend money
never being able to turn work down
oh, and on top of that, having to smile
all the bloody time
got to keep smiling

Best
Job
In
The
World

It doesn't appease him in the slightest
does he know it's not me he's angry at?
I hope he finds a calling he enjoys
that someday he comes to realise
it's the dealer who let him down
not the bloke who got blackjack

LP

My mother first gave it to me
that vast expanse of black plastic
bigger than both my little boy's hands together
brought to life with the lethal-sounding needle

I was entranced, fascinated, afraid
I knew it carried history and significance
contained the feelings and lives of many now gone
could unlock the secrets of everything

The names, Beatles, Stones and a mysterious man named Cat
were like ancient magic spells to conjure
escape, freedom, wisdom, endless potential
I could touch the universe from here

Packed in huge squares of beauty, images and words
secrets, codes, messages, dedications
hinted at the majesty, but never confirmed
proved more glorious mystery than information

As I endeavoured to set my head
precisely between my tiny, tinny speakers
to hear exactly as the sorcerer intended
the sound gigantic, fierce and everywhere

It felt like home, like protection
like being scooped up in the arms of the Almighty
This was mine; I learned how to find tracks and numbers
twelve, seven, forty five, thirty three and a half

Stories, songs of all and nothing
Scared by the surreal stream, I repeated
the words, and as I grew older
learned they meant less as I understood them more

Now I have learned to copy them
I produce shadows of The Shadows
and I make my own, in studios, on stages
but they seem to belong to me less

More Than Music (moment of Madness)

I need you more than my record collection
every scratch and jump and imperfection
I need you more than Snoop Dogg needs to swear
more than Britney Spears needs underwear
more than James Brown's need to funk
more than the Buzzcocks need for punk
more than Judge Dredd needs to be bawdy
more than Lindisfarne needs to be Geordie
more than Johnny Cash needs to drawl
more than Eminem needs to appal
more than Docherty needs a drug
more than Status Quo need to chug
more than Jagger's need to be skinny
more than Lulu needed her mini
more than Winehouse needs a whisky
more than Shaggy needs to be frisky
more than Glen Miller needed a dance
more than Tom Jones needs looser pants
more than Thom Yorke's need to moan
more than Queen's need to be overblown
more than the Spice Girls needed Posh
more than the Pogues could do with a wash
more than Ozzy's need to shock
more than Whitesnake's need to rock
more than Prince's need to be tiny
more than Morissey's need to be whiney
more than Zappa needs to be freaky
more than the Bee Gees need to be squeaky
and above all this, and deepest of all
more than Paul needed John, and John needed Paul

Inevitable

I have an innate hatred of patriotism
inane campaigns to add the flag to taxis
extra syllables grafted onto chanted place names
the wicked misuse of "British" by bigots
stories meant to reflect ancient glorious empire
told really to forgive current faults

Yet I am irrationally attached
to the lump of mud I live on
pride is a sin, and a mortal one at that
ashamed I struggle to name
this absurd affection for a collection
of buildings, bridges and rivers

The silly thing is it seems to love me back
the opposite of those steadily buzzing Kings Cross nerves
I know how it sounds - dewy-eyed local lad
or an old cloth-capped husk recounting glories
but it's not the mundane football song defiance of late
it's the homes, the lives, the work of generations

It breathes, this city, it breathes and speaks
it sings and shouts and paints and draws
it dances across the coal-scarred country
it gives me strength from its harrowed past
keeps me pounding towards a powerful future
shame faced, I celebrate this space, and all that it holds

Anti-sonnet

Oh how I hate you, your arrogant face
self-important voice, your withering stare
your counterfeit smile, your bogus embrace
your negative stance, superior air

The way you put down those better than you
belittle their effort, talent and zeal
look down on their bright young passion and skill
tell those around you how they should feel

I know you hold me in equal disdain
yet you are never that far from my side
to remain so close must cause you such pain
you already seem so dissatisfied

I was taught hate was wrong, a grave mortal sin
but I hate you, and I suppose that means you win

Smoking Poem

It's not so much the taste, it's the ritual I miss
from the buying through the fire to the long slow smoky kiss
my self-image as raconteur was nothing without wine
and a Marlboro in my hand, drawing just at the right time
smiling darkly through the cloud of poison and perfection
each witticism magnified by the dangerous confection

It's the marking out of time and the feeling of reward
the evening punctuated, never having to be bored
the sharing and partaking, every smoker chipping in
the communal light, regretting, and the promise to give in
the knowledge that we're all done for and death is our choice
accepting our mortality in gravel-deep cracked voice

Now I say I'm convinced that I don't want a cigarette
laugh at the friends who still indulge - outside and getting wet
I can see the strong defiance in the rain and in the cold
and the feeling of not caring, as they're never getting old
their insolence to stand up and blow smoke right in death's face
I realise it's my twenties, not my fags, I can't replace

One Night Two And A Half Weeks In

It's three AM
I know they're in the house
Four on the dressing table
one on the coffee table
three in a box on top of the fridge
two in my coat pocket
I can see them in my mind
That's almost half a pack
What a waste

Its' four now
The last thing I need is a stimulant
but it's the only thing
How much harm could one do?
I try to chant the magic words
Cancer, emphysema, strokes
but they seem a million miles off
and my craving is here
breathing in my face

Around five
I drifted off for a minute
the dream was magnificent
in the pub, new Year's eve '97
the gang were all around me
My friend who I was tragically in love with
her boyfriend, my best mate and my band
Like a scene from a channel four sitcom
the communal packet in the middle

She was wearing angel's wings
we were laughing and singing
it was rising to the heavens
floating up into the air
with every breath
we didn't care if we reached the millennium
or about what diseases would get us in the end
The gang and the moment
would never get old

Then I was awake
For a second I forgot
but just for a second
Then it was back
like the bloke who won't leave
at the end of the party
In the end I didn't do it
I shuffled off to bed
You see, giving up has no resolution

Break Up Calypso

Please come back for inadvisable sex
you know the type you only ever have with your ex?
our relationship has been a failure
but there's nothing quite like familiar genitalia
we can lie easy in the afternoon
in the faded sun of our abandoned room
forget why we ever split from each other
act like you were never my lover

Let's do things we wouldn't have done together
when you thought you'd have to look me in the eye forever
our inhibitions are a thing of the past,
asphyxiated by our romance's collapse
the pressure is gone, we can make love, laugh
not worry about who should be cleaning the bath
whether we have money, where we should be
it feels like when we just got together to me

This could be our last chance to drop our defences
before we eventually come to our senses
it's a joyfully regrettable mistake we can make
and share the awkward glances when we finally wake
this is all we have left, our last common ground
we'll have time for remorse when tomorrow comes 'round
it's time that we physically reminisced
let the past pass away, but the passion persist

Ode To Angry Environmentalist Poet

Where do you get the energy
to be so angry all the time?

If only we could harness
your uncompromising rhyme

Even when you're slightly narked
you project it with such passion

Isn't this a type of gas
we could recycle in some fashion?

We could combat global warming
and replace some fossil fuels

Your fury could light hospitals
council flats and several schools

If only we could channel it
into a power station

We'd have greener transatlantic flights
that run on agitation

So think of the bigger picture
before you start the revolution

Consider that your pissed-off prose
could be a carbon free solution

Note To Self- List Of Things Not To Write Poems About

1. How difficult it is to be a poet. Can't hack the constant pressure of which coffee to order next? Go and work in Woolworths'.

2. Tony Blair or George Bush. Both these subjects have reached their TVP, that is, Total Volume of Poems. It is impossible to write an original word about them. This also applies to globalisation, Iraq, the American dream, the environment, Big Brother and cats. (The animal, not the Andrew Lloyd-Webber Musical. NB- This does NOT mean it's ok to write about the Andrew Lloyd-Webber musical.)

3. Your home town and how wonderful it is. It's identical to the one fifty miles down the road. It has the same HMV, H&M, C&A, B&Q and BHS. It has the same fast food joints, ancient monuments and out of town shopping centre. The same amount of historical firsts happened in their town as in yours and their local celebrity is just as obscure as yours. Get over it.

4. Writer's block. Now that would be an original idea, wouldn't it?

5. Your girlfriend. You're going to feel pretty stupid after pouring your heart out on paper when you come home in six month's time to find that she's run off with a Scots guardsman called Jimmy, because he's a proper bloke and not some wishy-washy poet who spends all day and thirteen quid in Starbuck's writing four lines about how hard it is being so sensitive.

6. Your children or pets. Your baby looks like Winston Churchill if it's a boy or Ronnie Barker if it's a girl. Its cry is no more or less piercing, its emissions no more or less odorous than any other human child. Your Labrador looks and acts the same as any other Labrador who ever lived. They are made in a factory in Wales by ex-miners who were put out of work by Thatcher

7. Thatcher. See Bush and Blair.

8. Your first love. They have either forgotten you or laugh at you for not having a proper job. On a broader note, stop kidding yourself that poetry impresses girls. Football impresses girls, so does going to the gym, doing DIY and driving a massive car. Understanding the term iambic pentameter is somewhere on the list below crochet and having a fossil collection.

9. The following rhymes are illegal- Strife/Life, Together/Forever, You/Blue, Brother/Mother, Float/Boat, Love/Above, Only/Lonely, Crying/Dying, Feet/Street, Hips/Lips, Chance/Dance, Chlamydia/Get rid o' ya. (Actually, that last one is quite good).

10. Oh, and writing a list is not a poem. That's cheating.

On Me Ed

An obvious rhyme
didn't harm Lear
He used them all the time
no, he didn't fear
the glares of his peers
when repeating a line

I find his words move
us to laughter because
he was not out to prove
how clever he was
he wasn't looking
to his friends to approve

He wasn't concerned
with appearing bright
or being spurned
or ignored on the night
for not getting it right
or the praise he could earn

He was happy to write
nonsense, limericks
just keeping it light
with little word tricks
not concerned with cliques
on a poetry night

But then he never played
The Cumberland arms
nerves shattered and frayed
head filled with alarm
that he'd come to harm
from the poet brigade

So I don't claim to be
clever, witty or quick
I don't care, you see
if you condemn or pick
or if you think I'm thick
it won't matter to me

For if Ed gets away
with bong trees and boats
then I'm going to play
with lyrics and notes
'til I find what I wrote
might be fun to say

I suppose all this means
I can't be in your gang
who all seem quite mean
and like to harangue
with a sarcastic twang
and have uncertain hygiene

So forgive my cheek
but I'm off to rhyme
and avoid your critique
and not socially climb
but, just have a good time
with the words that I speak

See Vee

Your new employer wanted
a reference for you
I pushed all the right buttons
ticked all the boxes

Punctual, reliable
confident I lied
Is fine left alone I said
Completely untrue

On a reference
there is no room for
all the things that I wanted
the beautiful truth

No space for tears of concern
I saw you shed for
the emptiness of the lives
you saw around you

I could not write "powerful,
strong, shrewd and vulnerable
more than her slight years and frame
would ever tell you"

I don't think employers are
concerned you provide
my shelter in misery
ally in mischief

They won't need to hear of
the years of mistakes
we've forgiven each other
and laughed at later

And I'll probably leave out
that you have never
seen your own brilliant spark
lighting those you touch

"She'll be an asset to you"
I say honestly
and hope that one day
you can see it for yourself

Compère

Good evening, welcome to the show
tonight, a musical hero
indeed, a rock and roll maestro
a true melodic dynamo

His, a fearsome reputation
he's played in remote locations
toured abroad in many nations
graced TV and radio stations

He has inspired adulation
infatuation, procreation
caused his peers much frustration
at his rapid elevation

He creates magic audible
exceedingly recordable
his CDs are affordable
and musically laudable

Achieving immortality
through his polytonality
he's shunning all formality
to play in your locality

So, see the audience exclaim!
and see him set the stage aflame!
performer of extensive fame...
Oh Bugger – I forgot his name

Heated Conversation (An Exercise In Backwards Masking)

Scanning the room for compliments
I strain to overhear judgment
two pass the stage, I lean over
I hear a very strange sentence

" I don't know why he was so upset, I only set fire to him!"

It's not what I was looking for
but, at light-speed, in-between songs
I backwards engineer the words
right to the conversation's source

" I don't know why he was so upset, I only set fire to him!

You can see why he'd be annoyed though
It's not like I did it on purpose
Oh, well that wasn't very clever
I blew it hard in his direction
obviously. Very sensible.
I was putting the campfire out
Ok, then what happened?
No, hold on, it gets worse
So? Is he a veggie or something?
But, I cooked us breakfast to say sorry
That's not so bad, you've done worse to me
Yeah, I spilled lighter fluid on him
What happened, did you fall out with him?
Yeah, but, we're not friends since Glastonbury
Me too. Doesn't your mate teach guitar?
I wish I was talented like that
Yeah, and his songs are works of genius
That bloke on stage is a great singer"

Yeah, I'm sure that's how it went

James At The Job Centre

Here at the job centre
we'll get you back to work
since your untimely dismissal
how have you been, Mr Kirk?
we'll find gainful employment
that matches your skill set -
given the things you say you've done
I'm surprised we haven't yet

You say you have experience
of other cultures and their ways -
sometimes when you meet them
you don't shoot them for several days
your phaser's often set to stun
and your doctor is on hand
to kindly tend to all their wounds
when you punch them soon after you land

Throughout our little galaxy
you're respected and even feared
you get on well with your best friend
even though he's differently eared
so this portrait that's been painted
on your violent CV
of a xenophobic maniac
seems unjustified to me

On Monday at eight thirty
beam yourself to B & Q
meet the boss there, Mister Kahn
for an initial interview
while I'm on the subject
go unarmed to this one, yeah?
the manager of Woolworth's
is still in intensive care

Our only other option
is McDonalds on the fries
and that's not really fitting
for a Captain of enterprise
so put on your best Beatle boots
nylon tunic and a smile
boldly go, get off the dole
and onto the screwdriver aisle

On Beginnings

So

You shouldn't be timid
but don't be aggressive
slowly saunter up to it
confident nonchalance
look like you're excited
not like you're desperate
look bright and fresh faced
the thousandth time over
relaxed, but not passive
brand new but familiar
sound like you don't care
but like you do care
not like you do care
but not like you don't care
different, not outlandish
exactly as loud as
it needs to be, no more
cool, composed, but not bored
intoxicated, not drunk
breathe in the right place
smiling, not grinning
accessible this way
unreachable that way
satisfied, not smug
special, but ordinary
flawless, not threatening

Then sing your second note.

Automatic For The People

Welcome to Simpson inc. automated entertainment service
For songs, Press one
For poems, press two
For a witty retort to a heckler, press three

You have chosen songs
To hear a selection of our quality original material, press one
To hear a hand-picked assortment of cover- versions, press two

You have chosen cover versions
For poignant, press one
For sing--along, press two
For romantic, press three
For local, press four
For that one by that bloke, man, that one that they sing on that programme, you know, the one with the couple in it on the thing, press five

You have chosen sing-along
For a song from the fifties, press one
For a song from the sixties, press two
For a song from the seventies, press three
For a song from the nineties, press four
For a song from the eighties, please hang up and do not call again

You have chosen nineties
You want Wonderwall don't you?
You have been placed in a queue
Meanwhile, here is some music

The Day You Decided

Ten thirty AM, through watery sun
I come home from a triumphant broadcast
We fought last night, over a surprise present
I am, bleary-eyed, full of defiance

You said that you know what is best
Is that true?
You said that I could not decide
Is that true?
You called me pathetic again
Is that true?
I said "I don't care what you think"
Is that true?

I realise as soon as I see you
it hits like a double espresso
as you begin to speak, I know for sure
without question, how this morning will end

You say that it's not about me
Is that true?
You say there's no chance for reprieve
Is that true?
You made this decision yourself
Is that true?
It's about our future, not now
Is that true?

I don't know why, but I do not panic
though my defiance suffers instant death
Your sad, sure, solid, familiar tone
lets me know already there is no hope

You've tried really hard to mend me
Is that true?
I made no attempt to improve
Is that true?
I forgot the value of you
Is that true?
My soul has been lost in my past
Is that true?

Behind the thin disguise of suddenness
lie weeks of deliberation and thought
I do not argue with your decision
I simply begin to agree with you

I won't give you what you deserve
This is true
I rejected you constantly
This is true
I put everything before you
This is true
I always said that you'd leave me
This is true

As we both cry our tears are like children's
beyond our control and all reason
you recount once again all my failings
I, desperate, say how right you are

I'll never be more than I am
This is true
I never believed in the dream
This is true
I can't leave my weakness behind
This is true
I'm lost but I won't ask for help
This is true

You leave and I look at the door for hours
I sit and I begin to rationalise
You did what you had to and can't be blamed
I reason myself to sleep on the floor

Old Friends

We bump and you ask how I am
as politeness dictates you must
Happier than I've ever been"
I relate, all bright eyes and teeth
I love it, life is fantastic
I've so much to look forward to"
You smile, reply "That's great to hear"
I hope I was more convincing

Height / Polite

You are quite short
It must present difficulty
when you have to address
a tall man's chest
or adjust the seat
in every office you work in

I often wonder
if you think about it
but it seems rude to ask
and I am aware
you don't choose to be little
but I choose to be courteous

Have a Good Show

Have a good show mate
do your best and they'll love you
knock 'em dead.
well, within boundaries, not actual murder

but really, I wish you every success
well, maybe not *every* success
but the ones that won't make me jealous
I genuinely hope you can achieve

I want you to find what you're looking for
as long as I approve of your discovery
If I find that you have reached the peak before me
I'll have to renegotiate my journey

You see, every piece of praise you receive
is drawn from a finite praise bank
every round of applause you get
depletes the great cosmic lake of applause

When anyone gives you a compliment
it invalidates every single time anyone has ever told me I'm any
good at anything at all from riding a bike to kissing a girl, so please,
please fail miserably and publicly

But, you know, have a good show

Highland Conversation

"There's nothing else to do"
her eyes are not quite white
in the places that they should be and
are older than her smooth, skinny body

She'd been to a funeral
an eighteen year old friend
she insists she didn't do the bad stuff
just speed and coke and "that"

"There's nowhere else to go"
she tries to light up, but misses
she swears at the cigarette
viciously, as if it were a person

She laughed about the service
about the way they found her mate
after she'd been dead for three days
she laughed about the boyfriend crying

"There's nothing round here"
she gestures dismissively around
at the mountains, the bay, the boats
to illustrate their absence or invisibility

Looking down at her glass
the anger returns to her
she looks up at no one, face full of shadows
"I need another treble" she cries

The Drink

The hair of the dog is returning to bite you
in your cold bed you are starting to dream
morning is coming and daylight disturbs you
last night is coming back and you silence a scream
but you know the answer is clear and it's easy
tonight is a matter of hours away
and joy as the ritual comfort surrounds you
we'll be in the same place but we'll still run away

So take your pleasure, welcome every measure
come on, take your reward, live and die by this sword
take your choice, drinker raise your voice
are we really the masters anymore?

We drink to the fact that we're lonely but hopeful
drink to the hand we've been dealt with disdain
you need to cover impurities deeper
I need to blanket this fast tear stain
You know the easiest way we can solve it
temporarily but what do we care
this ancient and sociable drug of distinction
there's greater and grander and drunker out there

It's your joy it's your selfish destruction
it's temptation, redemption, seduction
It's the love of your life, it's your mother, your wife
and the drink will be my mistress evermore

Stop Kidding Yourself

It doesn't matter
No-one was looking
I'll always love you
You're looking lovely
I didn't mean it
I'll do it someday
Someone is out there
They didn't notice
It'll be alright in the end

Lie

We'll never break up
I like your new song
It's just a bad day
It's just the weather
It's not really your fault
I blame my parents
I'm mainly happy
I'm really complex
It'll be alright in the end

Lie

I'm really listening
You make me happy
No, I'm not jealous
I'd never judge you
I know you love me
I like your girlfriend
You're looking thinner
I've had a great time
It'll be alright in the end

Lie

Daytime In Darlo

The charity ones are the best, solid gold
cheerful daytime gigs when no-one quite gets it
why a man with a guitar and a cheap mic
is smiling and singing at them in the rain
A girl with a litre of oblivion
sits grinning on the teacup roundabout
nodding (and surprising rhythmically)
happily shouting "aye!" every time I stop

The wet unemployed, infirm and official
look on with an incredible joyful mix
of interest, concern and studied ignorance
"Can you sing Yesterday?" asks an old lady
I come back with "I can't even sing today!"
she doesn't get it, but then it makes me laugh
and despite everything and everything else
I quietly begin to enjoy myself

The sound man battles manfully (and soundly)
not to be electrocuted by his gear-
sound becomes a very secondary concern
toddlers do that "don't know why I'm moving" dance
a nurse on a tombola smiles right at me
as the bloke on the big wheel requests Elvis
Laughing I remember all of a sudden
that I have the best job in the entire world

One Down

If we met I'd have an answer

rehearsed, ready and nonchalant
every aspect ironed out
gone through a thousand times over
re-run like a classic film quote
every time we may just meet
the words even appear in dreams

Even though we miss each other
very subtly keeping apart
explaining it away with smiles
revealing nothing to our friends

Moments cannot be avoided
ever-vigilant though we are
every bump slightly less sad
telling our dates we're not hungry
indiscreet though it is to leave
not that I wouldn't know what to say
greetings, smiles, then my perfect line

you never ask though, I'll save it
or maybe it's best to one side
unsaid, left, in the margins

Meeting The Public

There comes a time
between first and second sets
when a performer must mingle with the audience
this is the moment when
my superpower activates
and my drunken philosopher magnet begins to work

It's almost a talent
they are drawn, almost dragged
inevitably, irreversibly, irresistibly
to the seat next to me
two inches too close

And I know I should feel lucky
because this fella knows the answer
To EVERYTHING in the UNIVERSE

Writing, he says, is not about books
it's not about producing or deadlines
music, he says, is not about performance
it's not about pleasing the masses
comedy, he says, is not about laughter
it's not about the funny things in life

I nod without eye contact
desperately scrabble in my brain
for every non-committal phrase I know

everyone has an opinion, I say
it's all about perspective, I say
depends how you look at it, I say
it's horses for courses, I say
It's a subjective subject, I say
It depends
maybe
could be
I see
Ok
ah
oh
mmhmmm...

SEE! he says, triumphantly
as if I've been converted
another naive youngster
shown the way to enlightenment
Oh lordy, he's on to politics now…

Politics, he says, is not about people
it's not going to make his life better
religion he says, is not about God
it's not about faith or morality
school, he says, is not about learning
it's not about improving anyone
the world, he says, is not about people
it's not about multi whatever it is

I take a long drag
and try to find something, anything
I can talk about without agreeing or disagreeing

This summer's been bad, I say
this is a canny boozer, I say
rain's coming on, I say
err.. Beatles are good
beer's.... nice

Beatles? He says, cannot stand them
this bar he says, has gone right downhill
the rain last year, he says, was proper rain
Is it not time you went back on?

I leap at the question
like a goalkeeper on trial day
leave half a cigarette
and run to the stage

First song, second set, about to start
I look back and see he's alone again
I wonder why the man with all the answers
has no-one to talk to but the singer

A person out of his element
vulnerable in a room of strangers
trying to get people on his side
spending every night in a pub
the same words to different people
putting himself across the only way he can
performing to stay alive

I look at him and he looks back
"This one's for you" I say
but it's really for me

Reality / Television

I saw you dance on the grass at Haymarket
like The Kids From Fame had been transplanted
and landed on a grey May day in Newcastle
enthusiasm and tans intact

I can see it now - U.S.T.V's in town
the A-Team fly by, reformed ex-pitmen
in an armour plated Blyth council wagon
soldiers of fortune and dominoes champions

To Cheers, a west-end boozer with curtains drawn
where everybody knows your name, and your Mam's
Frasier plays the bandit, doles out sage advice
every fitting an antique, and not by design

High above in the big flats by the shops
the Friends watch QVC and the racing
Ross smiles to Rachel "I'll be there for you"
as their giro finally arrives

I might not have the skyline or sunshine
sure resolutions or good moods
or the certainty of a happy ending
but at least my life doesn't break for adverts

The Committee

The committee who decide
where the matter should reside
met to discuss you
if you should continue

They will try to justify
debate, explain why
you deserve to be
is it better that you are?

What would there be in this room
if this volume wasn't used
to accommodate
this potential waste of space?

A brilliant new machine
or a thinker, a writer
inventor of things
physician, magician

This space doesn't have to be
you, a waste of energy
displacing the air
making the useful not there

And then they decide it
they imagine the freedom
possibilities
the endless bright potential

So your space must be taken
your existence made forfeit
Broken and useless
you're a waste of resources

Rest, now. You will not be missed
relieved they close up their lists
cross out your name
adjourn for tea and biscuits

Secret Track

I don't want to make your life a mess
I don't want to cause you pain
elopement is not in the air
I don't want to change your name
don't ever think the state we're in
is unfair or worse unkind
remember that at any time
I'm free to change your mind
don't think I'm dizzy with the drink
don't think I've thought this through
I don't want to drown you in despair but
I want to shake your canoe

I think it would be travesty
if we never went to bed
imagine the mad passion
and the mess inside your head
as we make our gladly blinded way
to the inevitable conclusion
I'll revel in the disarray
bathe in the confusion
I won't promise not to make you cry
with the wicked things we do
I don't really want to rock your boat but
I want to shake your canoe

I'm not a nice guy
I thought you'd worked that out by now

Physicians of Penzance
(for Doctor Liz)

I am the very model of a medical professional
I'll answer every question both physical and ethical
I know your body inside out from humerus to testicle
I'll cure that rash you caught from hippies at the Reading festival

I treat the truly sick and the clearly hypochondriacal
the resolutely sane also the clearly maniacal
I could have been a lawyer, but I felt I had a higher call
If a treatment ever fails I won't rest till I try them all

Of medical anatomy my knowledge is impeccable
I'll bring you back from critical until you're feeling quite stable
you've never been in safer hands than when you are on my table
If your waters break, fear not, I'm great with an umbilical

I love my work and take reward from helping to make you alright
but superhuman I am not, and time off is a human right
people often accost me to cure them of their every blight
so when I'm on a night out I say I work on a building site

In my work I can perform from remedy to miracle
I back this up with patient records, evidence empirical
but when I am off duty please don't mention matters clinical
Never forget
        I can kill you
                without leaving a mark

Judge Dread

Of course we all judge
You ask me not to but
I judge that
the fact that it worries you
tells me a lot

You can't judge a book by its cover
well, let's be honest, you can
If it has a picture of a lion a witch and a wardrobe
It's unlikely to be the new Harry Potter
(although it may have some suspiciously familiar themes)

You will judge me by
what I wear
what I weigh
what I say
what I don't
how I stand
where I stand
what I stand
what I can't

You will judge me by
the books I'm into
the music I'm into
the films I'm into
the drink I'm into
the magazines I'm into
who I've been into
and whether I still fancy them

You will judge me by
my favourite song
my favourite café
my favourite place
my favourite shoes
my favourite shows
my favourite jokes
my favourite smokes
and good lord in heaven above help me, my favourite Spice Girl

It's Sporty by the way

I will, in turn, judge you
by all of these measures
before you've had a chance
to tell me what to think of you
but maybe I'll like
your unmodified self
I might love all your failings
your quirks and your secrets
I might love all that's hidden
so get them out, be yourself
emotionally naked
bathing in the cold bracing waters of my prejudices
not caring what I see, I may just love it

Yeah, but
I'll be donning my metaphorical big black jumper
(And my physical one, actually)
hiding all the bits you may dislike
until I'm in the warm duvet of familiarity

Think of me what you will
but I'm not bloody stupid

Backbone

I met you in a café
I wasn't really sure
I only sat down at your table
to avoid a draughty door
Your mineral water sparkled
sadly not your conversation
I should have mentioned straight away
that I had my reservations
but you gave me your phone number
to refuse it would be rude
so I rang you on my break next day
asked you out for food

As an alternative to boredom
it was a satisfactory meal
not having to make an effort
had a strange kind of appeal
I didn't like your clothes or shoes
I didn't like your hair
but to mention it at that point
well, it would have been unfair
I didn't argue with you when
you said you'd pay the bill
so I decided not to say right then
that your perfume made me ill

I was feeling slightly guilty
as you'd taken me to town
so I rang you on the Saturday
to take you out and let you down
I suggested that we'd get some drinks
I could summon up the guts
to tell you, you weren't right for me
hoped you wouldn't make a fuss
but once I'd had a rum and coke
your face looked slightly better
so I spent just one more evening
and decided on a letter

I was sitting typing slowly
when you rang me on the phone
saying that you'd had a bad day
didn't want to be alone
I claimed that I was busy
But the guilt was kicking in
so I said I'd pop round later
with some sympathy and gin
but people being people
one thing led us to another
and in a post-orgasmic haze
I agreed to meet your mother

I thought I'd give it one more month
now that I'd met your folks
I didn't want your Dad to think
I was one of those bad blokes
but then it was your birthday
then Christmas, Valentine
I couldn't really split with you
at such a special time
then you planned a holiday
you'd already booked the plane
before I realised it
it was birthday time again

It's easy to forget some things
when you're into a routine
that fiddly little box of pills
the week gaps in between
It's not like I regret the twins
now they're starting to calm down
I just miss my morning lie - ins
and my Friday nights in town
so I resolved to set it straight
just as soon as it was right
to tell you that I never loved you
just not on a sleepless night

The Wedding was in August
it was such a stressful day
I considered backing out of it
or coming out as gay
but what would people think of me?
I only tried to do my best
to keep everybody happy
I never wanted all the rest
so now I have my bed made
that's the story of my wife
and how breaking strength of backbone
can have impact on your life